Letters from Ines ... *Dear Eva*

by Ines Lindblom

Translated and edited by Karin Hokkanen
All hymns and passages are translated from Swedish

NORTHWESTERN PUBLISHING HOUSE
Milwaukee, Wisconsin

Cover photo of Eva Söderström
Back cover photo of Ines Lindblom

Library of Congress Control Number: 2002108324
Northwestern Publishing House
1250 N. 113th St., Milwaukee, WI 53226-3284
www.nph.net
© 2003 Northwestern Publishing House
Published 2003
Printed in the United States of America
ISBN 0-8100-1487-4

Contents

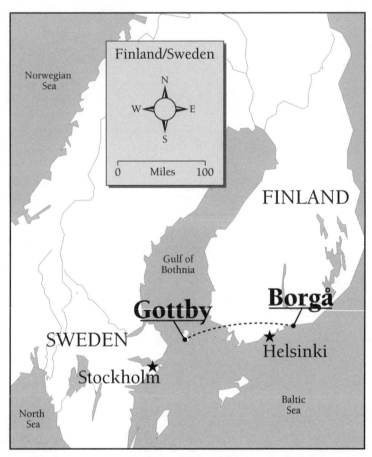

Living over 100 miles from each other are two dear friends.
Ines Lindblom lives in Gottby, and Eva Söderström lives in
Borgå, Finland.

Introduction

Finding a handwritten letter in the mailbox can be both a surprise and a high point of my day's activities. The letter shows that someone, somewhere, is thinking about me; however, personal letters do not just arrive from an anonymous someone, but from someone who both knows me and genuinely cares about my welfare. What a pleasure to read the words sliding fresh from an envelope, and what a greater blessing to reread those same words of encouragement and affection days and weeks afterward.

Letters from Ines . . . Dear Eva is a timeless, inspirational collection of letters from one Christian friend to another. Ines Lindblom, now in her nineties, lives in Gottby, a small village outside of Mariehamn on the island of Åland in the archipelago between Finland and Sweden. Eva Söderström, a few years older than Ines, lives in Borgå, about 40 miles east of Helsinki, Finland. The two women became acquainted at a conference for the Scandinavian Lutheran Confessional Church during the mid-1980's and quickly discovered their bond of faith in Jesus. Although isolated by age and distance, they developed a special friendship over the years through the exchange of letters, cassettes, phone calls, and an occasional cross-country visit.

I first met Ines in her flower garden when I was bicycle-touring from Finland to Sweden by way of the Åland islands. Although I did not speak Swedish at the time, Ines opened her home and showed hospitality to a young foreign traveler.

Coincidentally, more than a dozen years later, while visiting friends in Finland, I stopped for a few days to see Eva, whom I had met at church while I lived in Finland. Age differences melted away during the long afternoons over the never-ending cups of coffee, as I listened to Eva's stories peppered with the humor and practical wisdom that come with the blessing of years. One afternoon, Eva brought out a thick bundle of letters wrapped with a rubber band. "You should read these letters from Ines," she said, handing me the stack. And so I began reading through the years of carefully preserved letters—the same ones presented here that you will soon read—that are as inspirational and encouraging today as the day they were written.

Letters from Ines . . . Dear Eva gives us messages from the heart of a Christian woman who lets all of us know that we are not alone in the world. No matter where we live, no matter what language we speak, no matter what our backgrounds—we are united by the common bond of saving faith in Jesus who died for our sins. *Letters from Ines* is a celebration of the faith and friendship that connects us all.

A heartfelt thanks to Eva Söderström, who first shared her friend's letters, and to Ines Lindblom, who gave kind permission to translate the letters she wrote into English. Thanks also to Jukka Söderström, pastor in the Finnish Lutheran Confessional Church, who helped with photo-copying the original letters.

Karin Hokkanen
Mankato, MN
June 2001

Letters from Ines

Gottby ~ Sunday afternoon ~ October 13, 1991 ⊠ 1 ⊠

Dear old friends in Borgå,

A heartfelt thanks, Eva, for the letter with the cassette. With all my heart, I thank God for your friendship in faith in our Lord and Savior Jesus Christ. Thank the good Lord for Eva and Pecki! Thank the good Lord for Jukka who is our souls' shepherd on earth. Today on this delightful Sabbath day, we've again received the opportunity to be grounded in God's rich and inexhaustible Word. Thanks be to the good Lord who allows us to have our thoughts so clear that we can still grasp some of these riches. In addition to the cassette, Luther's sermon about Jesus' parable on wedding clothes was spiritually enlightening, as usual.

We've had a dense fog for several days. No flights were able to land, so the mail was delayed. Today's a bit clearer to see the best of all right now, the beautiful fall colors. I picked a bouquet of dahlias this morning. We haven't had a frost here yet, and today I picked the rest of the Victoria plums.

Warm greetings to you both,

Ines

Dear friends in faith,

A heartfelt thanks, Eva, for the cassettes. I'll send the one you want back later. Thank you! Thank you! What spiritual teaching—especially the connection between the Old Testament and the New Testament! Those tapes are worth listening to several times.

I'll soon write to our friends in Västerås, Sweden and remind them of our desire to have them make an Åland trip this summer. My God, give us all health and energy so that we can once again gather at my place.

Jukka's visit, as always, was edifying. Just as the physical bread is important so the body can live, so the spiritual bread (God's Word) is just as important for the soul to live. Every day we need this bread. In John 6:48 Jesus says, "I am the bread of life." Thanks be to the good Lord for the living spiritual bread!

> I need you, O Jesus,
> Out of your fellowship alone
> What abundance I receive.

Yesterday we received about four inches (10 cm) of snow in the morning, the most we've had this winter, but today the snow is almost gone. We've had the spring sun very sparingly, so we need to pray to God for a warm spring sun.

The pain in my arms is quite a bit better. I've visited three different doctors who say that more movement is necessary. Outside work at a slow pace would be helpful.

I hope God gives you both satisfactory health for the body, because with our age we can't be like young people.

Heart-warm greetings,
Ines

Dear old friends,

A heartfelt thanks for the telephone call, as good as always, and spiritually encouraging. Yesterday we had a reminder of Christ's transfiguration up on the mountain. What comfort for the disciples to be able to see something of that heavenly glory, already here on earth, and hear the voice of God the Father saying, "This is my beloved Son! Listen to Him!" What great comfort for us who believe in God, in Jesus, because it reminds us of the Sabbath rest that awaits God's people. "Oh blessed peace, to believe in Jesus and have God's Word at home."

Jukka had a lot of good things to tell in addition to the sermon and the Lord's Supper. There was such good spiritual fellowship at the annual conference. It is God's grace that unites his children as one in faith.

Jukka's sermon on Cain and Abel was particularly good and instructional. Abel is reminiscent of Jesus as the Good Shepherd and Cain as the sinful human race. Cain confessed his sin and said, "My sin is greater than what can be forgiven." Just think, already God's forgiveness was there for those first people. God's Word is so rich; God's Holy Spirit opens hearts to the heavenly treasures in the Holy Book.

It's already August, and the summer is getting toward its end. We should thank God for the delightful season that he gives us through grace.

We've also had rain with storms and unpleasant weather, 100 mm (4 inches) in one day.

Loving greetings,

Ines

PS Thanks ahead of time for the cassettes.

Dear friends in faith,

Thanks for your phone call and the new number. I haven't been able to call now for some time. Once again, we've celebrated the Sabbath Day, Sunday, to Jesus' glory. Each one of us, no matter where we live, should take for herself those heavenly rights—God's living Word that stands forever. My thoughts have been with the closing of the annual conference in Gothenburg, Sweden. We can thank God. We who are old and unable to travel so far still have the Word at home on cassettes and in books. "The grass withers and the flowers fall, but the word of our God stands forever" (Isaiah 40:8). All flesh is grass.

It's clouding up some and maybe God will finally allow the much needed rain. For seven or eight weeks I've watered almost every night just to keep the plants alive. All of Scandinavia is suffering from drought now except way up in the north. We don't know God's purpose with everything around us.

I wonder if you were at Jukka and Anja's son's wedding? He told me about it on his last visit.

Loving greetings,

Ines

Dear friends,

A heartfelt thanks for the telephone call. Just as always, it's encouraging to be able to talk to friends in the faith. The same doctrine and confession unites God's children as one already here on earth.

Today, once again, we've been able to celebrate the Sabbath Day to God's glory. According to Hebrews, there will be a Sabbath rest for God's people in heaven. No sorrow or sin or imperfection shall rule there. Thanks be to the good Lord!

> No eye has seen,
> no ear has heard,
> no mind has conceived
> what God has prepared for those who love him.
>
> (1 Corinthians 2:9)

Fall approaches now with its dark mornings and evenings; the month of August is at its end. How time flies! We've had a warm and delightful summer. After the long dry period, we had a span of rain in the middle of harvest time. There'll be poor quality grain of whatever is left after drying. The potatoes are rotting in the ground after all the continuous rain, and the government in Finland is decreasing the growing acreage for the farmers. We have too much of everything. But God will take care of things even if there is a smaller harvest this year.

We have plenty of plums and apples. They're all ripening early this year on account of the warmer summer.

I'm sending a card of Åland's small churches. Of course,

they're beautiful and elaborate, but oh, how spiritually poor. Number 11 is my old church. Nowadays they are renovating the church for three million marks (about half a million dollars) for a few poor souls who visit there on Sundays. That money could have been enough for food to feed many hungry people in the world.

Loving greetings,
Ines

 Gottby ~ October 4, 1992

Dear friends in Borgå,

A warm thanks for the beautiful card with your loving greetings. I can imagine the card is from Holland, the land of flower bulbs. What rich colors God our great Creator lets the children of men enjoy. Thanks be to the good Lord for everything!

Today is Michael's day, the children and angels' day. I read, among other things, Luther's sermon about those who don't accept God's kingdom as a child does. They will never get to the kingdom. Thanks be to the good Lord for the great mercy of being God's holy children here on earth.

> Think, how wonderful to be a child of God
> A bride by his Son's blood dearly bought
> When your final rest comes near
> Rejoice, child of God, that time has passed.

I've had help indoors and out with fall cleaning and clean-up of the flower beds. At a recent doctor's visit, he said I should avoid this kind of work as much as possible since my back and all its tendons are very worn. If nothing helps now, I'll go for some physical therapy later. I thank God for every passing day. "So I take only one day at a time, and do not fear the morning that dawns."

God has sent me two young men who believe in God. The one is a well-educated, intelligent, twenty-eight-year-old man. He is a self-taught cantor, without a church. He holds organ concerts where he plays the music of Bach. He sometimes teaches Latin and German at the Åbo Academy, as well as being an artist. He is so humble, trusting in God, and he willingly comes both to help me with different chores and talk on spiritual matters.

The other boy, twenty-one years old, might be a little sickly with his nerves, but happy and affectionate even though he comes from a divorced household. He is alone and nobody cares about him. This is a big part of my thanksgiving, a large gift of God. I feel my smallness and great unworthiness when I think about the grace I have received from the Lord, to talk about God and his Son's work with these young men.

Warm greetings,

Ines

Gottby ~ November 18, 1992

Dear friends in Borgå,

Once again God has let us experience a new day of grace. Thanks be to the good Lord! "By grace you have been saved, through faith . . . it is the gift of God" (Ephesians 2:8).

I wish and hope God gives you both the strength to take care of your home in the future. And just think, God gives us much more than what we can pray for or think of. I am so glad and thankful to God that you both are alive and still on the earth. You both have meant so much to me spiritually. There are so few true friends of the heart.

It was nice to hear from Jukka that the summer in Uppsala, Sweden felt so warm and good with the Spirit's fellowship. The Lord blesses us in our own spots! This coming Sunday we celebrate the church year's last Sunday, Judgment Sunday. It reminds us that the Lord is coming to judge the earth. He will come from the sky just as the disciples saw him ascend. That big day is coming no matter what. May we be like those wise virgins with oil in their lamps when the shout is heard, "See, the bridegroom comes!" The day and moment no one knows, not even the angels in heaven, only the Father alone.

The postcard of the sea eagle is just a little greeting from a friend who often thinks of you both.

Ines

 8   *Gottby ~ December 9, 1992*

Dear friends Eva and Pecki,

With greetings from friends, I wish you both a good and peaceful Christmas in the fellowship of Jesus. Without the baby Jesus in Bethlehem, born for our sakes to take away all the world's sins, there would be no Christmas to celebrate. Along with the heavenly host's chorus, we join in the angels' song on Christmas night "Glory to God in the highest, and on earth peace to men on whom his favor rests" (Luke 2:14).

The time goes so quickly; we don't have long left until that big, festive day. But the Lord helps us day after day.

The cassette recordings you sent are, as always, very spiritually encouraging. The sound quality isn't the best; I had to have my hearing aid on the highest setting to hear. Then I could understand every word.

I'll try to call you today to see if I can hear better with the telephone. Usually I can hear quite well with the connection to Helsinki.

We've had good weather now for a while, calm and above freezing. The ground is completely green here, and the winter period in October doesn't seem to have done any great damage.

We have reason to thank, praise, and give glory to our heavenly Father who has so graciously allowed us to have life so good—materially speaking. Out in the world there's so much need, unrest, and above all, suffering. May God be merciful to us and all people.

Warmest Christmas greetings,
Ines

Gottby ~ April 25, 1993

Dear friend Eva,

A warm thanks for the telephone call yesterday. It's always so pleasant to talk with you because Jesus' fellowship unites us. I think about how lonely you are now without Pecki, so many empty rooms in that big house. But we have a great gift from God as long as we have our own thoughts clear, are able to manage with our daily chores, and can be in our own dear homes on earth—as long, anyway, until the Lord calls us home to heaven. What delight and happiness we have to thank God for.

Today we had the Good Shepherd's Sunday. The text from John chapter 10 is about the Good Shepherd, and Luther gave good instruction in his sermon today. "I [the Good Shepherd] will search for the lost and bring back the strays. I will bind up the injured and strengthen the weak" (Ezekiel 34:16). The book of John talks often about the hired hands whom the sheep don't recognize. When a hired hand sees the wolf coming, he abandons the sheep and escapes. When I think about the state church in our day, I begin to wonder if there even exists a proper shepherd who seeks the lost sheep. May God protect us in our own true faith in the Word that is God, according to John's first chapter. We have every reason to have gratitude toward God who daily protects us from all the temptations that flood the whole world. "Surely goodness and love will follow me [you] . . . and I [you] will dwell in the house of the LORD forever" (Psalm 23:6).

Warm greetings from Ines

Dear Eva,

A day of grace has once again dawned. The delightful spring sun warms everything and the flowers are blooming in countless numbers. The plants grow so quickly with this heat. I hope you feel quite well and can enjoy the warmth without Pecki. He is home with the Lord Jesus and everything is good with him.

Here comes a cassette that's just as educational as always, with the biblically clear gospel for the poor, sinful children of men.

I wait and hope every day for Jukka to call and come for a visit. Was he maybe in Borgå yesterday?

I'm not exactly well; there's more ache in my arms and legs and I fall easily. "Praise be to the Lord, to God our Savior, who daily bears our burdens" (Psalm 68:19).

Warm spring greetings from Ines

Dear friend Eva,

A sincere, warm thank you for the telephone call yesterday evening. It's always good and encouraging to be able to talk to and meet a friend of the Lord Jesus who has the same faith, teaching, and confession. Even though we are so distantly separated from each other, we are able to meet in the Word—through faith, by grace. The Word is

God according to John chapter 1. Thank God, who lets us wake up to a new day of grace. Thank God, who lets us get up every morning. We can be grateful that we are able to live at home, in our own homes, as long as God wills it. All this is by grace and a gift from our dear heavenly Father.

Following my Bible reading list, I just read Deuteronomy chapter 8 that tells about the Lord's kindness to his people during the desert wandering. We have the same God and Father yet today. Eva, read Deuteronomy chapter 8 as a warm greeting from me.

It was saddening to hear what you told about that one man. The devil has great power and wrath. If possible, he tries to lead away every single person. But the *Lord Jesus is the stronger one* who has won victory over sin, death, the devil, and the world. The one who believes in the Son has life and teaches the Word. We are blessed and saved by grace. Thanks be to the good Lord! May we be protected in the living faith of our Lord and Savior!

Even the Word teaches that all nature sighs and is in agony for deliverance. We've had strange weather. The whole of May was unnaturally warm with severe dryness, and now it's cold and rainy with frost at night. I hope you've received some rain now. Yesterday it was only +5C (42F), today +7C (45F) and cloudy. We see plainly how the Lord leads and directs the weather and winds.

Loving greetings,
Ines

Dear friend and Sister-in-Faith Eva,

Thanks, thank you for the telephone call and some additional glimpses from the annual conference. As the hymn says, "How delightful, oh Jesus, While we walk scattered here in the world, We have the company of the Spirit; Yes, mutual companions on the journey with all who travel to Zion (heaven)." And also "Then I see God's Lamb, who has bled for me here And thank and praise my dear Savior . . . " Just think, when we go to heaven we'll be able to see God's Lamb, the Lord Jesus, in the middle of the large multitude of all the redeemed and all the angel choirs. We'll no longer be lonely like we are on earth.

What great grace, Eva, that you are so spry and able to hear well. My hearing has gone down somewhat more in the last year. It's hard for me to learn with the hearing aid that's supposed to be a remedy. On the other hand, I see well. The Lord gives us individually what we need. The time we have remaining on earth can't be so much longer, when we both are so old.

Lately I've been reading, among other things, the book of Jeremiah. What teaching! We have the same God and Lord today as in Jeremiah's time. The prophet Jeremiah was sent by the Lord to preach judgment on the impenitent Israel. What suffering Jeremiah had to endure! The Word burned like a fire in his heart; he had to tell the truth. "O LORD, my strength and my fortress, my refuge in time of distress" (Jeremiah 16:19). Jeremiah experienced those attributes of God in full measure. Even we can experience the same, we who believe in the Lord Jesus.

No doubt we see with distress how our country's archbishop spiritually leads Finland's people to destruction. His latest speech on homosexuality reveals this waywardness. May the Lord God support and protect us, his little remnant, by grace for Jesus' sake.

The archbishop's statement is nothing less than the theology of reason. "'They are prophesying lies to you in my name. I have not sent them,' declares the LORD" (Jeremiah 29:9).

"The heart is deceitful above all things and beyond cure. Who can understand it? 'I the LORD search the heart and examine the mind, to reward a man according to his conduct, according to what his deeds deserve'" (Jeremiah 17:9,10).

Forgive my lines, Eva.

Loving greetings,

Ines

 13 *Gottby ~ October 7, 1993*

Dear friend Eva, in faith united to the One,

A warm thanks for the telephone call yesterday—what a lovely surprise! I'll send you Psalm 91 as a greeting: "Safety under the Most High's shelter." I started the day with this wonderful psalm. We don't need to be afraid of anything. "I will say of the LORD, 'He is my refuge and my fortress, my God, in whom I trust'" (Psalm 91:2). The Lord himself and his holy angels protect us from all evil. Yes, "I will protect him" in verse 14. Thank the good Lord for his precious, dear Word that we can go to in our loneliness—for then we are never alone.

> When I in faith my Jesus see
> Dear to my heart let Him be—
> His heart for me stands open—
> There I hide both body and soul
> And live so heartily well.

What do we old people need more than Jesus, our Lord and Savior? Day by day and moment by moment, he is near us. He abundantly gives whatever we need. Thank you!

The fall is truly here. What wonderful colors nature clothes itself in! God gives everything by sheer grace and love to us fallen children of men. In weakness I even thank God for my little home that has light and warmth as the darkness tightens over the land and sea.

I understand that you miss Pecki, maybe even more now during the dark time of the year. But Pecki is at home with the Lord! What a delightful thought!

These are just a few lines as a little greeting,

Your friend Ines

Gottby ~ January 14, 1994

Dear friend Eva,

"Look, the Lamb of God, who takes away the sin of the world" (John 1:29).

> See God's Lamb, see Jesus' heart
> See how He offers himself

For your (and my) sin he felt death's pain
Dear soul, all this for me (and you).

The cassette sermon by Jukka, the latest one, was on
this text about Jesus when he was baptized by John. It was
a good and comfort-filled sermon as always. This morning
I read Matthew chapter 14, the chapter with John's
beheading, among other things. This forerunner of Jesus
received such a shameful death because of an irresponsible
girl. The Lord's way is truly strange. Here we can be
ashamed; we can't understand anything of God's greatness.

Thanks, Eva, for your latest telephone conversation. I
think about you often, so often, all those days when I'm
sitting alone. How good that we can be together in faith and
spirit. Every day I've been listening to the cassette lectures
on the prophet Isaiah—sixteen cassettes, thirty-two lectures.
They are all so rich in teaching. I said on the phone that there
were eight cassettes, but there are double as many, sixteen.
Jukka should get them after me, but in the meantime, I don't
know where they'll end up after my death—unless we get
some more time from the Lord our God.

The darkness over our earth is tightening even more.
Difficult devastations of different kinds are happening,
even fire in Australia. Mankind's ungodliness only grows.
It comes closer to the goal every minute. But the goal for
us is heaven, where we all can see Jesus, in whom we have
believed. Lord, help us by grace and mercy so that we
might not die on the way home. There should be a small
remnant when the Lord comes, according to God's Word.
The prophet Isaiah talks about how only a little group shall
exist, a small remnant of grace for the sake of Jesus Christ.

We have the presidential election on Sunday. We can sigh and pray to God for the right person. Little is spoken of our land, our fosterland, and how to protect it.

Forgive my lines, Eva. I probably tire you out with my scribblings.

Warm greetings,

Ines

Gottby ~ May 2, 1994

Dear Eva,

> "Rejoice that your names are written in heaven"
> (Luke 10:20).

Yesterday I listened to Jukka's sermon a few times. What a good sermon, beautiful song, and music. Seldom do we get to hear that fine a song from Sweden. It helped the above Bible words become so alive for me. We can rejoice and thank God who by grace lets us poor sinners know and rejoice that our names are written in heaven. Thank the good Lord! "I am not ashamed of the gospel, because it is the power of God for the salvation of everyone who believes" (Romans 1:16).

> We don't see each other
> but nevertheless meet constantly
> with the dear cross . . .

Thank you, thank you, dear Eva, for the latest telephone call. It's edifying to hear a friend who has the same faith, teaching, and confession. Thanks be to God that Eva, Jukka, and Anja are there. Likewise, Jukka's brother who plays the piano so nicely. The music gilds the service.

Today is the third day in a row of a northern storm and only +2/+3 degrees warmth (33-34F). That's part of spring on Åland, with the icy north winds. The ice in the Bothnian Sea has been so thick this year, 1 meter, as we've heard on the radio. As the storm loosens the ice, we hope it goes toward the south to eventually melt.

Anyhow, God has been so gracious that the ground has become green and a portion of the spring bulbs are blooming. I feel the storms with aches in my whole body, but after it's calm, I'll be better again and can be outside a little.

Loving greetings. I hope you can read these lines.

Ines

16 *Gottby ~ Monday morning ~ May 30, 1994*

Dear Eva,

We have a new day and new grace by our dear Lord and Savior. Thank you, thank you, Eva, for the call Saturday afternoon. We have much to thank God for every day and moment, above all, that we have our thoughts clear so that we know what we say and do.

I began reading Luther's sermon (12 pages long) yesterday on the Holy Trinity. What teaching! The text was John 3:1-15. It was about Nicodemus who came to Jesus at night. In spite of his learning and exemplary life, Nicodemus was lacking the most important thing, to be blessed by grace by being born again through water and the Spirit (Baptism). Jesus says, "You are Israel's teacher . . . and you do not understand these things?" (John 3:10). Many teachers in our time are like Nicodemus and have not been born again. Thanks be to God for the gift of eternal life. Read John 3:16.

This morning the temperature was +5C (39F) and cloudy. There's no warmth yet; the north wind continues with the chill. Nevertheless, we got more rain yesterday, and we can thank God for that. The weathermen promise warmer weather to come from Sweden after a few days.

I'm sending the cassette to Jukka today, to be sure we will be able to enjoy the gifts God gave to us sinful people. The whole of nature, as it were, rejoices and praises God for these gifts of beauty.

A few incomplete lines with loving greetings from Ines.

Gottby ~ August 7, 1994

Dear friend Eva,

God's grace and peace surround you!

A heartwarming thanks for the cassette. What a surprise to listen to Jukka's sermon that he told at my house several years ago. I remember so well those precious moments at my home. Yes, I remember that we sang "Oh, blessed moments that Jesus gives us . . . ." I tried to set the radio volume on fairly high so I could hear Jukka's sermon on the rich man and Lazarus. It was as consoling as always for us poor sinful people. Thank the good Lord that we, in our very last times, are able to listen once again to that life-giving gospel on sin and grace.

> The world is so full of dangers on the Way,
> Oh, this one is so narrow.
> And of Satan's many snares,
> Counting never reaches full measure.

Just from our little sister church in Sweden we can see how Satan and human reasoning reign among the members. Instead, people should just fall down before God's face and pray for forgiveness; we are sinners, all of us, and sin daily in our thoughts and actions. We can pray that *Christ's love* for us sinners may be placed in every heart, and we also can and should thank God for that indescribable grace we enjoy daily. "Oh blessed peace, to believe in Jesus and have God's Word at home."

Now you have, dear Eva, waited a long time for some thanks from me. The almost intolerable heat this past week has made it impossible for me to write. The air was unusually humid and everything indoors was damp. The windows and door must stand open in order for me to be able to breathe. Thank God that we've now had cooler weather and some rain also. Today it was +18C (65F) and cloudy. In Borgå you may have had even warmer weather, but with less humidity. We have the sea close by here.

I was glad for the visit of Jukka and Anja, and in spite of the heat, I managed to make some simple food, etc. The little devotion time that Jukka held in the morning gave good spiritual food for the day. God gives us everything as a loan and gift of grace as long as we remain here in this

20

perishable world. We can only thank and praise God, our Lord and Savior. The following song verse came to my mind this morning:

> It is finished! so Jesus said
> On the cross' stem. All the world's sinful guilt
> The Father laid upon this Lamb.
> For love he took it upon himself
> And fully paid for you and me.

So when God's Spirit writes this truth in our hearts, we can be glad; yes, we can't do anything except thank our heavenly Father who has arranged everything so well. "The blind receive sight, the lame walk, those who have leprosy are cured, the deaf hear, the dead are raised, and the good news is preached to the poor" (Luke 7:22). We can already taste some of that peace which surpasses our understanding.

Read hymn 112 in the hymnal sometime as a warm greeting from Ines.

Gottby ~ September 18, 1994

Dear Eva, friend in Jesus Christ's grace,

Thank you, thank you for the telephone call and the cassette. How great is God's grace that lets us have our thoughts clear and in our full possession so we can hear and read God's Word; it is life giving and powerful for the soul! Today I've listened twice to the good and comforting sermon for us unworthy sinners. May Jesus' words "Ephata, open up" press into our hearts daily. They remind us that every day and moment we *can* know of our sins' forgiveness by the sake of Jesus Christ.

I hope that you are feeling fairly well. I thought that your voice on the telephone sounded tired, maybe more tired than usual. We are, of course, becoming older with every day that goes by.

> May the years gladly fly
> Only let Jesus be my friend
> His word is my (and your) lantern
> That enlightens you, my friend . . .

For each and every one of us our years and days are tallied by the Lord Jesus. "If we live, we live to the Lord; and if we die, we die to the Lord. So, whether we live or die, we belong to the Lord" (Romans 14:8). That's a delightful promise out of the Holy Book. "By grace you have been saved . . . it is the gift of God" from Ephesians 2:8.

This coming Thursday I'll have X rays of my back taken. Then it will probably take an additional week before I get the opinion from the doctor, since that doctor has office hours only two days a week. Only when I am careful with work does my back feel any better. Day after day the Lord helps in large and small things. Thanks be to the dear Lord for caring for us.

Fall is coming closer all the time. No frost yet, just a lot of rain and storms in between.

These are a few lines with warm greetings,

Ines

Dear Eva,

> Blessed are those who have learned
>> to acclaim you,
> who walk in the light of your presence,
>> O LORD.
> They rejoice in your name all day long;
> they exult in your righteousness.
> For you are their glory and strength,
> and by your favor you exalt our horn.
> Indeed, our shield belongs to the LORD,
> Our king to the Holy One of Israel.

(Psalm 89:15-18)

Thank you, thank you for the telephone call this past week. It was a great joy and comfort for me to be able to talk with a true friend of Jesus. The above written words of the 89th psalm give me nourishment. The Holy Spirit reminds us that all of God's Word is equally valuable. Sometimes it's one verse here and sometimes another verse there that fills the heart with blessed comfort and peace.

Thanks, Eva, for the beautiful card "The Good Shepherd." Every day and moment he bears us in his arms. What a faithful Shepherd we have! If I cannot believe this every moment because of that inherent heart-depraving sin, Jesus is always the same anyway.

What shall I say about the changes in the confession of sins in the cassette package? The contents in itself are just the same, but I would prefer to read the old version that our Christian forefathers wrote. Morning and evening, yes, sometimes more often, the confession of sins comes to mind. I need it unchanged. I'll talk to Jukka about the revision when he comes.

We have fall now and the wonderful, beautiful colors that God gives us in nature. I wonder if you understand my lines that are probably inarticulate at times.

Loving greetings,

Ines

 Gottby ~ November 22, 1994

Dear Eva,

Thank you, thank you for the happy greetings from the land of sun and flowers. There people don't need to pay for heat like we do in the cold north. We thank God, in any case, for our birthplace and our fosterland, Finland. "Our country, our country, our fosterland . . ." wrote J. L. Runeberg, a Finnish poet.

Yesterday is past. Tomorrow we haven't yet seen. Today the Lord helps us. These are delightful words for a poor sinful person.

Jukka is expected here around the second advent. His previous visit was so beneficial to me. I think every day about how deep in God's Word he is; it's a great gift from God to research the Holy Scriptures that are inexhaustible. I'm glad that Jukka is my pastor.

"[He] daily bears our burdens. Our God is a God who saves" (Psalm 68:19,20).

By grace I live, by grace I die,
By grace I come in to the city (heaven).
See, this is reason enough for me to stand
And sing Hallelujah forever.

These are a few hasty lines with warm greetings from a sister in faith.

Ines

My dear friend Eva,

Thank you for the cassette with the affectionate greetings, Eva! The sermon was good, as usual, since Jukka was preaching. Alvar Svensson's Christmas sermon was one of the best I've heard from Sweden, and the recording was good.

Today I read Isaiah chapter 35 about the Lord's redeemed people returning to Zion, the home of the Savior, the Lord Jesus. Just think, Eva, there is a blessed road called the holy way for us who believe in the Lord Jesus. A redeemed people will travel on that road—we who believe in Jesus, in his suffering, death, and resurrection for the sake of all our sins. All of this is only by grace upon grace. Think how we already have life through faith and then, "gladness and joy will overtake them, and sorrow and sighing will flee away" (Isaiah 35:10).

On Friday, January 12, Jukka came to visit, and the time was as always spiritually uplifting with discussion, a sermon, and the Lord's Supper. The sermon this time was about the prophet Jonah in the whale's belly, an account that so clearly and obviously shows us Jesus' suffering, death, and resurrection.

Day after day, the Lord helps us. We've had a strange winter with above freezing temperatures every day. All the snow is gone. It's so good that the dark time will soon be over and the days will be brighter and longer. We old folks content ourselves in these blessings of the Lord's goodness, if only we could always be thankful. I hope you, Eva, are spry for your 90th celebration.

Warm greetings,

Ines

 Gottby ~ February 26, 1995

Dear friend Eva,

A warm thank-you for all the greetings in the cassette package. Today we have Shrove Sunday and with that we are in Lent. "See, we go up to Jerusalem in the holy Lenten time. To behold Jesus Christ, God's Son suffering in place of sinners." We can spiritually follow Jesus on that painful journey up Golgotha to die for yours, mine, and all the world's sins. How few even consider this in our time! May God protect us, keep us firm with the Word, God's Word, which is living and powerful. Many temptations are inviting in our day. The church that's called Lutheran isn't Lutheran anymore except in name, and Catholicism spreads more and more. The Savior says, "Let me find faith on earth toward the spirit." We who live now probably live close to the Lord's return.

Last Monday Jukka visited, and the time was, as always, just as encouraging around the Word. Furthermore, we had the Lord's Holy Supper for our forgiveness of sins.

Today I heard Jukka's cassette sermon from Borgå. I miss Lasse who almost always played piano the past number of times. But what can be better than to be home with the Lord?

Quite soon you'll be ready to fly to Västerås, Sweden. Already now, I'll wish you a good trip knowing that it will be a spiritually beneficial journey. God's grace and peace be with you on the trip.

"Look, the Lamb of God, who takes away the sin of the world!" (John 1:29).

Warm greetings,

Ines

Gottby ~ Monday morning ~ April 10, 1995 🖂 23 🖂

Dear Eva,

"Praise be to the Lord, to God our Savior, who daily bears our burdens" (Psalm 68:19). I want to wish you a good and happy continuation of Holy Week, and also of Good Friday and Easter. Only the fellowship with Jesus gives true and genuine happiness. I recently read Isaiah chapter 53, that wonderful chapter on Jesus' suffering and death. What a miracle that the prophet Isaiah could prophesy this 750 years before. "But he was pierced for our transgressions, he was crushed for our iniquities; the punishment that *brought us peace* was upon him, and by his wounds we are healed" (Isaiah 53:5). Oh what love, wonderful, true. Never has anyone loved as he.

What a great blessing of God Jesus has prepared for us through his suffering and painful death on Golgotha's cross. Now during Holy Week, we can follow Jesus in faith on that oppressive, painful road. All this was for you and me. It was *our sins* he bore.

Jesus didn't remain in the grave. "He is risen, rejoice my soul" from one song. With all God's children, no matter where we live or how we have life, we can only thank God and sing:

> Up my tongue, to sing praise
> To the Hero who on the cross' stem,
> For us bled, suffered and died
> Like a harmless sacrificial lamb.
> Out of the grave according to the Scriptures,
> He now in glory steps forth.

Dear Eva, you will certainly celebrate Easter with one of your children, perhaps they'll come home to visit you. On Good Friday, two of my brothers-in-law have birthdays, one is eighty-five, the other seventy-five years old. In between, I'm at home and have life good with the Word.

Warm Easter greetings,

Ines

Good morning, dear Eva,

We have a new day and new grace of the Lord. Often, often, I think of you, but am slow to write a few lines. It's so good that we are included in God's almighty protection no matter where we live and how life goes. I was reading in God's Word, Isaiah 43:1-3.

> Fear not, for I have redeemed you; I have summoned you by name; you are mine. When you pass through the waters, I will be with you; and when you pass through the rivers, they will not sweep over you. When you walk through the fire, you will not be burned; the flames will not set you ablaze. For I am the LORD, your God, the Holy One of Israel, your Savior . . .

What comforting words for us poor sinful people! We have it good, Eva; we can be glad that our names are written in heaven. "If the faith and body are weak, the treasure can yet heal me, won by Christ alone . . . " It was precisely the weak and wretched people full of imperfections that the Lord Jesus took on himself, not the clever, self-pious ones who didn't need the Savior Jesus Christ.

This morning we have a thick fog. I wonder if the flights with the mail are still able to come? Maybe it will clear up later in the day. Yesterday we had 20 mm (almost 1 in.) of rain. The plants grow luxuriously, to say nothing of the weeds.

I'm somewhat better with the urinary infection, but am tired, so tired. I thank God for every day that goes by, that I can still be on my own and take care of myself. I hope you, dear Eva, are as active and as smart as always.

Warm greetings,

Ines

 Gottby ~ July 31, 1995

Dear Eva,

Thank you, thank you for the letter in the cassette package. "Surely I am with you always, to the very end of the age" (Matthew 28:20). What words of comfort for us sinners—the Lord Jesus is with us! We are able to live by the forgiveness of sins every day and moment. May God protect us from the devil who goes around seeking those he can swallow up.

Think, dear Eva, blessed by grace! It's a miracle of God that we will be able to meet once more on Åland. You will be welcomed in Jesus' name.

Right now we have a strong heat wave; here it was up to +26C (78F) in the shade. Mostly, I sit inside, since I suffer some in the heat. I hope for cooler weather when Seth, Brigitta, Evan, and Jukka come. If God wills, I'll meet you with a car on Friday morning, August 11.

Warm greetings and a likewise welcome,

Ines

Dear Eva,

"Look, the Lamb of God, who takes away the sin of the world!" (John 1:29).

A warm greeting to you with the above words, a delightful verse for us poor sinners! Again and again these words have come into my thoughts in the past few days—full of comfort, full of peace. Grace upon grace! Eva, we are part of that little body who believes and is certain that Jesus died for each of us as individuals in the world.

We had a good time with Carl and Ulla—spiritual fellowship in full measure. Carl was really moved when I said at their departure that if we don't meet again here on earth, then we will meet in heaven where we will be able to see Jesus as he is.

In addition, they had many photographs from their daughter's wedding on June 17 of this year. Next year they're planning a trip to America. They had so much to tell about the congregations they visited.

Already, I'm thinking about that unforgettable visit by you and the Erlandsson family. If God wills and we can arrange a time next summer, I'd enjoy that kind of meeting again.

Thank you, thank you, Eva, for the letter in the last cassette.

We have fine and beautiful weather, real fall weather, but with a severe dryness. Last night there was frost, so the dahlias froze.

Loving greetings from Ines

Dear Eva,

Thank you, thank you for the telephone call. I think often, so often, about you. But you have children and grandchildren who come and visit. Besides, we are never alone when we have the Lord Jesus as a guest. He is with us every day in the living and powerful Word.

Now during the weekend, God's Word has been abundantly close to us. Luther is a matchless master of teaching. I read sermons by him both days. What grace of God to have access to the Word! Between readings I listen to cassettes, so time never gets long. The days seem to run away and soon we are at home with God, especially since we who are so old cannot have such a long road left. When we are then home with God, together we can glorify and praise the Lamb along with the white-clad crowd—with the blessed who have gone home before us.

> Think, when for once I will be without sin,
> Free from my evil flesh and Satan's tricks.
> When all my thoughts are pure and clear
> And all my deeds are without blemish.

> Think once again, when with renewed eyes
> I will see Him in whom I've believed
> And prayed to and followed; imagine, on high
> Eternally blessed in His presence I will stand.

We must pray for grace that God will allow Ulrik to live and be restored to health. The Lutheran Confessional Church is so little and we need each other, even if the congregation in Ljunby, Sweden is fairly large. It's nice that they asked Jukka to Umeå, Sweden again since they have a real lack of guest teachers there. God bless them in Umeå. What a great mercy from God that we're able to have our thoughts clear. So many, many people don't know where they are.

Some warm greetings,

Ines

Gottby ~ January 7, 1996

Dear friend Eva,

Continued good wishes for the new year, 1996!

We've already gotten through one week of the new year. "Jesus Christ is the same yesterday and today and forever" (Hebrews 13:8). It's good and richly comforting to know that we can close out the old year with the forgiveness of sins. Because Jesus is the same, in faith we know that every day we can own "the forgiveness of sins, in accordance with the riches of God's grace" (Ephesians 1:7).

> I don't know what I shall meet
> In the coming year,
> For my eyes, God hung a lamp
> Whose light I can't ignore.
>
> I can't see a hand in front of me,
> But I know that the Lord is near,
> And high over breaking waves
> The trembling child he bears.
>
> Lutheran hymnal

We are having an incredibly beautiful winter with some sun for a little while nearly every day. And now the length of light is increasing a few minutes every day. We had a white

Christmas with glimmering hoarfrost; how great and gracious God is with us sinners. Today it was a little milder, only -1C (31F), with cold, blustery winds from the southeast.

I also have great gratitude toward God for all material goods: food and drink, water and heat. Everything has functioned well for me up to this point, and I'm really well off with the store and bank nearby. Even so, I feel my great unworthiness. The Lord God gives far more than we can pray for or even think of.

Thanks for your phone call. I've thought often of you and our brothers and sisters in faith around the world. God bless them all for his own sake during the new year.

Warm new year's greetings,

Ines

PS Thanks for all of the greetings with the cassettes!

 Gottby ~ March 3, 1996

Dear friend Eva,

Grace and Peace!

We are in the middle of the holy Lenten time recalling Jesus' suffering and death for the whole world's sins. "Oh what love, miraculous, true. Never has anyone loved like He . . . " The burden of sin was so heavy to bear that Jesus sweat blood in the Garden of Gethsemane. We can't understand anything of Jesus' boundless suffering, but we can in our weakness believe and receive everything by grace.

In Isaiah 53:4,5 we read: "Surely he took up our infirmities and carried our sorrows, yet we considered him stricken by God, smitten by him, and afflicted. But he was pierced for our transgressions, he was crushed for our iniquities; the punishment that brought us peace was upon him, and by his wounds we are healed." Thank you, dear Lord and Savior for this blessing, yes, grace upon grace.

Thanks, Eva, for all the greetings in the cassette package. I hope your strength has come back after that difficult stomach infection. We can take merely one day, one eye blink at a time. The sun is beginning to feel warm, but the air is cold. At night it's still below freezing; tonight -6C (21F) is expected.

I haven't gotten any flu bug yet. My hearing is somewhat worse, in my opinion, and the ear doctor can't do anything about it other than recommend a hearing aid. Otherwise, I'm about the same healthwise. God's Word that is living and powerful holds me up. Thanks be to God! The days run away quickly, but I don't know where the time goes.

Warm greetings,
Ines

Gottby ~ March 31, 1996

Dear friend Eva,

Thanks for the greetings with the cassette. Perhaps you received my greetings through Jukka who was here last Friday. We had an edifying time with the sermon, the Lord's Holy Supper, and the spiritual discussion. "The Lord outdoes himself." He gives us spiritually and physically more, yes, far more, than we are even capable of thinking about or praying for. The sermon was about the Lord's blessing according to the books of Moses and an exposition of the Trinity: the Father, the Son, and the Holy Spirit. What a treasure we have in the Word, that Holy Book. May we be driven by the Spirit to abundantly read and contemplate the Word more. I feel sluggish myself and guilty many times. Therefore, the Lord God imposes needs or sorrows of different sorts. Through these our dear Savior is able to draw us ever closer and closer until at last we can see him as he is. I sang a stanza of a song from my early youth for Jukka that I had heard a preacher sing: "It is you and I who are wretched and weak who are loved by the living God."

Holy Week begins tomorrow morning, Monday, and we read devotions, one for every day of Jesus' suffering and death. Thanks be to the good Lord for this precious truth. It was for our sins that Jesus suffered and died, for yours and mine.

> "It is finished," he (Jesus) finally said
> So he erased all guilt.
> Those believing this are blessed.

Today I read a sermon of Luther's on the Lord's Holy Supper. What a teaching master Luther is!

Warm Easter greetings,
Ines

Dear Eva,

   A warm thanks for the beautiful card with the wonderful
cactus flowers and the letter on the reverse side. What a
powerful and spiritually nourishing sermon Jukka held in
Borgå for the cassette mission. That was the same sermon
Jukka had here the last time. Thanks be to God for the
pure, life-giving gospel we get to listen to. The world is
so full of dangers, even in the spiritual realm; Satan goes
around searching for whom he can swallow up. All the
signs promise the Lord's return soon.

   The Word for the day comes as a greeting in Psalm
37:39,40: "The salvation of the righteous comes from the
LORD; he is their stronghold in time of trouble. The LORD
helps them and delivers them; he delivers them from the
wicked and saves them, because they take refuge in him."

   Yes, I've really been thinking about how we might all get
together for a festive meeting once more at my home with
Jukka, Eva, and Seth's family as last year. My hearing was
somewhat worse this winter, but otherwise I'm about the
same as always, but tired in between everything. It's fun to
be outside and to be able to pick a bit of everything, since
our good God has let us experience spring again. The
spring bulbs are blooming abundantly already. We had less
snow than usual here, and one week of sun and warmth
has hurried up all of nature.

   Has Jukka come home from America yet? I'll write to
the Erlandsson family soon and ask if they will make the

trip here again. If we live and God wills so, maybe it will
be possible. Maybe Marita could also come?

Warm greetings,

Ines

 Gottby ~ May 17, 1996

Dear Eva,

A warm thanks for the cassettes and your dear little letter.
The Spirit's fellowship through faith unites us already here
on earth, so that later at home with God in heaven we can
together see Jesus and thank and praise him for all eternity.

Jukka told how strong faith's fellowship was among our
brothers in faith far away in America. There were brothers
in faith from 14 countries, almost from around the whole
world. God's Spirit unites us by the Word, but God's Word
doesn't exist only of words, but also of *power.* Jukka's trip
was truly beneficial and encouraging for him. We are just
of so few members in Finland.

I'll write to Västerås today to hear if they are planning
to visit me this summer. Just think, if we could all gather
together again with a sermon from Jukka and the Lord's
Holy Supper, we should pray to God about this. Sunday,
Jukka had a good, deep sermon (the cassette sermon) on
prayer and so powerfully reminded us of this, "For where
two or three come together in my name, there am I with
them" (Matthew 18:20). Yes, the Lord is near us in the
Word that is among us every single day.

Yesterday, in faith we were reminded of when Jesus was

taken up to heaven. And he shall come again to earth in the same way as he traveled to heaven. Thank the good Lord for the life-giving Word! Jukka should be visiting Borgå on Ascension Day.

After several warm days, we received chilly weather again. Spring is late this year, and the rain is needed so much for our dry ground.

Loving greetings,

Ines

Gottby ~ July 21, 1996

Dear Eva,

"Give thanks to the LORD, for he is good; his love endures forever. Let the redeemed of the LORD say this—those he redeemed from the hand of the foe, those he gathered from the lands, from east and west, from north and south" (Psalm 107:1-3).

Today on Transfiguration Day, God's Word in Mark 9:7 says "This is my Son, whom I love. Listen to him!" What delightful words for us poor sinners. *Listen to him, take him to heart,* and be filled with the blessed peace and joy that Jesus took away all sin and guilt. "Free are we, he keeps sin far from us…" as one song goes. Oh, blessed peace, to believe in Jesus and have God's Word at home.

Thank you, thank you, Eva, for the phone call that touched me with great joy, to know that in our country there yet exists a band that will proclaim God's Word pure and clear. They are a little group that can teach sinners about the way to heaven. Thank the good Lord, our dear heavenly Father, for this blessing. It was great news to hear that Ola Österbacka was along. Now I'm waiting to hear more when Jukka comes for a visit. With pleasure I look forward to the day when you, Eva, and the Erlandsson family can come—if God so wills. "Everything rests in my Father's hands."

I hope God gives you health so we can once more meet here on earth.

Warm greetings from Ines

 Gottby ~ September 22, 1996

Dear friend Eva,

A heartfelt thanks for the greeting in the cassette and for the telephone call. Today is the Lord's Day, Sunday—to the Lord's honor. Today the church service is celebrated at your home in Borgå, and I'm with you in thoughts.

We had a good time here at home when Jukka came last Wednesday. We had a discussion, a sermon, and the Lord's Supper. The Lord provides us poor sinners with the life-giving Word that God's Holy Spirit drives to the heart through God's grace and mercy. Without the Word, there is no Spirit. Jukka recalled so comfortingly the story about the widow's son. All help seemed lost for the widow when both her husband and son were taken away by death. Everything often looks dark in spiritual matters. We are so cold, dead, and removed from God. But then we find help with the Lord Jesus—he gives us the Word. In it we find help in time of need, just like the widow. Jesus needed to say just one word to her. What authority and power in the Word! And Jesus is the same even today. We have the same powerful Word. Thanks. Thanks be to the good Lord and Father in heaven!

Rejoice, rejoice, you purchased soul
See, up there everything is well!
God is reconciled (appeased), satisfied,
That's a reason for a joyful heart.
And everything not understood now
You will be able to truly see
And with awe exclaim
Oh, what love he has for me.

Warm greetings,
Ines

Gottby ~ Sunday afternoon ~ October 13, 1996 35

Dear Eva,

I often think about you. Today I heard Jukka's sermon about the widow's son in Nain. Thanks for the cassette and the greeting from you that was inside. That cassette sermon was one Jukka had told at my place. It's a powerful, encouraging sermon that poor sinners need to hear. How well you all sang, Anja and Marita and Eva together with Jukka.

I wonder if Jukka was in Borgå today? I'm waiting for him to come here soon. My health is about the same, not that we can expect much better. Age takes its toll. I hope you can be as active as always. We have reason to thank God for every day and moment. Thanks to him we manage to get up out of bed in the morning and have our thoughts clear.

I had a problem with my teeth last week—my dentures broke. They should be ready this coming week. If Jukka thought to come, I hope he can push the date up to the following week or the week after that.

We have autumn here. But those grand colors on the trees will soon be at their end. We've had three fall storms already, and so many trees are bare of leaves.

I read Luther's sermon today. The text told of when Jesus healed a paralyzed man. It's so comforting when Jesus says, "Your sins are forgiven." What powerful words! The same words are said to all of us for the forgiveness of sins, through Jesus Christ. Thanks be to the good Lord that every day we have life and can live in the forgiveness of sins.

Warm greetings,

Ines

36   *Gottby ~ Sunday afternoon ~ November 3, 1996*

Dear Eva,

A warm thanks for the cassette. In Borgå you all have gathered for a church service and communion. I'll be able to listen to the service later on cassette. Jukka called up one day at the beginning of last week, and they're planning to travel to Värnamo, Sweden first, then come here for a visit bringing greetings from Sweden and Borgå.

Eva, maybe you have been to Pecki's grave with flowers on All Saints' Day? Today I've listened to a sermon by Seth on David's Psalm 111 and a lecture on the topic of "David's Fallen House." Both were given in Norrköping, Sweden many years ago. The trouble in David's house was very disappointing with such a hasty end. Unfathomable! How Satan can cause trouble! What does God mean with all that happens? We don't know. But at home with God, everything will be made clear.

I hope your health is fairly good. I've been to the dentist eight times, and now my teeth feel good. This is one of God's gifts to me. My hearing has gotten worse this fall. I must use the hearing aid when I listen to a cassette, but even so, it's hard to understand sometimes. I see well with my eyes and read instead. Thank the good Lord for eyesight!

Today we had sunshine and +10C (51F). Until now, there's only been a little rain for the dried-out ground. The Lord God gives us what we need. Tomorrow someone is coming to help me rake leaves.

Loving greetings from Ines

Gottby ~ Tuesday ~ November 19, 1996

Dear Eva,

I listened to the lectures by Seth that are always so instructional about the Old Testament. Jukka has asked me to send them to you. You will have a visit soon that is spiritually uplifting in the loneliness. No, we are not alone. The Lord is with us every day and moment.

Thanks for the cassette with your greetings that came yesterday (Monday). I haven't yet had time to listen to Jukka's sermon.

This coming Sunday, Judgment Sunday, the last of the church year's holy days, reminds us of the Last Day when the Lord will come from the sky to hold judgment. He comes as a thief in the night. Serious business! May we be found with oil in our lamps as it is written: Watch for the bridegroom! It is only by God's grace and mercy alone that we are protected in the true faith. And then, "An eternity with Jesus, and everything, yes, everything will be good."

> My (and your) future is light and long
> Beyond the restraint of time
> There God and the Lamb blissful I see
> And distress shall be no more.

Warm greetings,

Ines

 Gottby ~ December 8, 1996

Dear Eva,

> Rejoice greatly, O Daughter of Zion!
> Shout, Daughter of Jerusalem!
> See, your king comes to you,
> righteous and having salvation,
> gentle and riding on a donkey,
> on a colt, the foal of a donkey.

(Zechariah 9:9)

We are now in the middle of the holy advent season, which means we wait for Christmas, Jesus' birth. Just imagine, the prophet Zechariah received the blessing, the manifestation from God, to be able to foresee this event several hundred years before Jesus was born. Thank the good Lord that we live in this time after Jesus was born, suffered, and died for our sins, and yes, the whole world's sins! With the prophet we can be glad and rejoice over the gift of Jesus, and by grace believe and take him to heart.

> Gently, mild and good
> He gives the weak courage.
> Great grace He has to lead
> The one to be his bride . . .

It is we who are Jesus' bride and can receive him, grace beyond grace.

The telephone discussion about the lecture day in Helsinki was really gratifying. Thank the dear Lord that Stefan Sjöqvist will be there for all the lecture days. I pray for God's richest blessings.

I hope you are as spritely as always. We have had an unusually mild and good fall this year and there's no snow or even frost yet. We did get a lot of rain that was badly needed for the dried-out ground. My water barrels are always filled with clean water.

I was with a sister on Independence Day and we watched TV (I don't have a television). It was festive; the sermon was completely in Finnish by the bishop in Kuopio.

Loving Advent greetings,

Ines

PS Thanks for the note in the cassette packet.

Dear Eva,

Merry Christmas and a Good New Year in Jesus' name!

"Praise be to the Lord . . . who daily bears our burdens" (Psalm 68:19).

May God, by grace, let us old ones celebrate Christmas yet one more time on earth. In the Word, God comes close to us with his Spirit, and Jukka reminds us often of this.

I read today that wonderful chapter 4 of John about that Samaritan woman Jesus spoke with at the well of Sychar. It was Jesus who could give her the living water; she would never get thirsty throughout eternity. The woman knew that the Messiah would come and when he came he would explain everything to them. Just think, Jesus said to her, "I who speak to you am he" (John 4:26).

Now comes Jesus, our dear Savior, to each and every one of us at this advent and Christmas time. He says, "I (Jesus) who speak to you am he." Just like the Samaritan woman, we can be glad and rejoice in faith over Jesus who came and was born as a human being to redeem all sinful mankind. Praise be to God!

You will celebrate Christmas with your children and grandchildren, of course.

We have winter and cold weather, and now Christmas snow! The mild weather ended so quickly.

Please don't call me. It's a good telephone connection to Borgå, but with my lowered hearing ability, it's a little hard to understand every word you say. Thanks be to God that I see well. I hope your health is pretty good.

Warm Christmas greetings,

Ines .

Dear Eva,

"Yesterday is past, tomorrow you haven't seen. Today the Lord helps."

Thank you, thank you, dear Eva, for your help with the telephone number. Everything changes in our world, but Jesus Christ is the same. I hope that you are well in the future. This stomach flu is quite troublesome, with a few muscle aches in the whole body. It'll probably be hard on the old people, but maybe it's not so difficult in the Borgå area. No fever comes along with it. I'm glad Jukka could push up his visit to January 15th. We don't know where all this trouble comes from. There are so many poisons in the air, yes, even in the food.

We have much to thank God for, warm houses when so many people are freezing in southern Europe. And in some places in America people drown in flood waters. Even these different kinds of afflictions are signs of the last times. False spirituality spreads out even more. Jesus' word is true: "May I find faith on earth" when he comes to judge the living and dead. "Precious Jesus, keep me ready to meet you every moment . . ." With the Lord there is grace and plenty of forgiveness.

I'm sending you 100 marks (about $20) for the telephone call you made for my sake. I know you help me for Jesus Christ's sake, but we live in an expensive time. Food is not so costly, but everything else is. We have life good in our land, with an overabundance of everything. Because of this, people forget the Lord God; previously, it was during the war's disasters that many turned to the Lord God.

Warm greetings,

Ines

 Gottby ~ January 26, 1997

Dear friend Eva,

A hearty thanks for the telephone call. The Spirit's fellowship unites God's children as one. Think, dear Eva, we are encircled in Jesus' grace and peace already here on our sinful earth! Thanks be to the good Lord, our precious God and Savior, who surrounds each and every one of us with his hands! Soon we old ones are at home with Jesus in our heavenly home. And then we'll have an eternity with Jesus and everything, yes, everything will be good.

> Now I am content,
> Toward home will I now hasten,
> And whatever happens to me,
> I will nevertheless find rest,
> In Jesus' death,
> In Jesus' deep wounds,
> There I will be well,
> I a poor wretched sheep.

As always, Jukka's visit was good. The sermon from Epiphany was on Jesus as the light of the world and on John chapter 8 about the adulteress. In chapter 8 of John, Jesus wrote on the ground with his finger, to us, for knowledge and teaching. God's Word is so rich and comforting. It is stronger than a two-edged sword and goes through soul and spirit, marrow and bone, according to Hebrews.

I read in Saturday's Helsinki paper that bishop Erik Vikström criticized the orthodox pastors in Helsinki's Markus' congregation, Halvar Sandell and Henrik Parrat. Sandell was at the workshop course before Christmas with the theologians. Those who trust in the Lord will not come to shame, but persecution will come to Jesus' friends at all times. And not least in the very last times. We await Jesus' return at any moment. "Lord, hold us ready to meet you every moment."

Warm greetings,
Ines

Gottby ~ February 20, 1997

Dear Eva,

"Praise be to the Lord, to God our Savior, who daily bears our burdens" (Psalm 68:19).

A warm thanks for the telephone call and the greeting I found with the cassette. I promised to write a few lines and send you Jukka's sermon. This week it's been one thing after another, including a family from Ekenäs on sport break who lived nearby and came to visit me for several days. After this kind of visit, I'm tired in the evenings.

So here's how Jukka writes for rich spiritual encouragement: "The LORD will reply to them: 'I am sending you *grain*, new *wine* and *oil*, enough to satisfy you fully; never again will I make you an object of scorn to the nations'" (Joel 2:19).

The Lord has truly fulfilled his promise and has sent us:

Grain—that true wheat bread, Jesus' precious body as sacrifice for our sins . . .

Wine—that same drink, Jesus' precious blood as a sacrifice for our sins . . .

Oil—the Holy Spirit that burns with divine flames in the Word and lights up our dark hearts, and in which we have been anointed to be prophets, kings, and priests in the heavenly kingdom.

That's what Jukka writes.

What treasures in the Word! Yes, God's Word is living and powerful and goes through marrow and bone.

God feeds his own in the spiritual desert. Åland is, in a spiritual way, a desert. I have seldom been so spiritually uplifted as in Jukka's letter. I'll send you a copy.

Just think, Eva! It's altogether too much that we, by grace, are part of the group of prophets, kings, and priests. We must believe as the Word teaches and be blessed, for everything is by grace, by the sake of Jesus Christ.

Warm greetings,
Ines

 Gottby ~ March 23, 1997

Dear Eva,

Thank you for the card with the Easter greeting in with the cassette package. In connection with the holy week we are now entering, we gladly remember "the Savior's cross and suffering, as the Lamb was sacrificed for the sake of the world, for your sins and mine." The prophet Isaiah reminds us of this in his 53rd chapter, among others, "He was pierced for our transgressions, he was crushed for our iniquities" (Isaiah 53:5). Oh what love, wonderful truth. Never has anyone loved as he.

> It is finished he said at the end
> So he struck all guilt away
> He who believes this is blessed.

After a taste of spring, we received winter again. The spring bulbs that had peeked up out of the ground now look frozen. We'll have to wait a while longer for spring. The weather and winds have power in God's hands. The Lord Jesus gives us what we need even physically. The light is one of God's great gifts. The sun warms and shines so nicely in between the clouds.

Loving greetings,

Ines

Gottby ~ April 15, 1997

Dear Eva,

"And surely I am with you always, to the very end of the age" (Matthew 28:20).

This was one of Jesus' last greetings to his disciples shortly before he ascended into heaven. What comfort and security for us who believe in Jesus, the Savior! Jesus Christ is the same. The Lord Jesus is with us every day and moment wherever we are, wherever we live, no matter what our life's conditions may be.

Last Sunday we celebrated the Good Shepherd Sunday. Luther's sermon is very satisfying and comprehensive. "For it is by grace you have been saved, through faith—and this not from yourselves, it is the gift of God" (Ephesians 2:8).

> How blessed to find rest
> As a child in Jesus' arms
> Saved from need and danger
> And sing only of his name.
>
> How blessed to be led
> By his Spirit good
> And be daily cleansed
> By his precious blood.

The winter is still holding out, and spring is still going to have to wait. God steers the weather and winds, and again today we had a storm from the north. We have had several difficult storms recently.

Jukka is in Germany now, if all went as planned. He'll make a trip here on April 27th, if God wills.

Thanks for the phone call.

Warm greetings from Åland,
Ines

Dear friend Eva,

"Give thanks to the LORD, for he is good; his love endures forever. Let the redeemed of the LORD say this . . ." (Psalm 107:1,2).

A new day and a new week have again begun; a new day is a great blessing of the Lord. Thanks for the telephone call and the greetings I found in the cassette packet. In the midst of all the swirls in the world, and not in the least in the spiritual realm, you can come across someone here or there who will believe in Jesus and discover peace, joy, and tranquility in him who has died and risen for the sake of the world's justice.

Last Wednesday, at 8:40 A.M., I happened to listen to Ola Österbacka's morning devotion. He read from Romans 8:32. What a good and comforting sermon! "Everything is finished," he said at the end. Jesus won the victory and "in his victory we have courage. We have life in his blood, and from his sacred wounds we have continual exultation. Behold, we live by grace until we stand in heaven." Then we sang from the hymnal, "Jesus is my friend, the best whose like can never be found . . ." Just think, there is still someone who preaches God's pure and clear Word on the radio!

Today we have chilly weather again with a northern storm. The birches have gotten "mouse-ears" anyway. Everything is green; everywhere there's delightful greenery with the flowers. Here, Eva, you are able to see all that is blooming right now. There are four kinds of flowers on my slope, and spring herbs and orchids on the road to Mariehamn.

Wishing you warm spring greetings,
Ines

Gottby ~ June 15, 1997

Dear Eva,

> Sabbath day, how lovely you are
> Given by God, I hold you dear . . .

I send you, Eva, a little midsummer greeting in such a delightful time of the year, as nature awakes. What incomprehensible joy God has prepared for us again! We must think, praise, and sing joyfully to our Creator who gives us sinful people so much good.

Three weeks from today our little congregation will gather here at my home, if God so wills. If only we could once again meet here on earth. But the time remaining is short, especially for us aged old folks.

Thanks for the cassette! The text for the day is the parable of the lost sheep and how the Good Shepherd, Jesus, seeks a person until he or she is again found. We are the Savior's property, one and all, dearly paid for with Jesus' blood.

In the last few days I have read the prophet Isaiah's 41st chapter, along with some other ones, according to my old Bible reading list. What a consoling chapter. Thanks be to the good Lord for the life-giving Word!

You'll most certainly be celebrating midsummer's weekend with your children and grandchildren.

Warm greetings from Ines

Gottby ~ Sunday afternoon ~ August 17, 1997

Dear Eva,

A warm thank you for all the great telephone conversations with stories from your days in Vasa. Even now in Finland, our dear fatherland, there is only a little group that will follow the Lord Jesus according to the Word, God's Word, which is living and powerful.

Today my thoughts have been with you all in Borgå as you are gathered for a church service. Jukka will soon visit me, according to his phone call yesterday.

One day I read David's delightful Psalm 16:6, "The boundary lines have fallen for me in pleasant places; surely I have a delightful inheritance." Read the whole psalm, Eva, as a dear greeting from me. God's Word holds me up every day here in the loneliness. Where else should I go? Oh, I meet people every day, but I am alone in a spiritual way. "The LORD is close to the brokenhearted and saves those who are crushed in spirit" (Psalm 34:18).

We've had nearly intolerable heat this summer. Again today it's a few degrees over +20C (68 F). In any case the nights have been chilly and longer. We're heading toward autumn.

"Only one day, one eye blink at a time . . ."

Loving greetings from Ines

Gottby ~ Sunday afternoon ~ September 21, 1997 48

Dear Eva,

Thanks for the greetings in the cassette. I listened to both yesterday, and today I listened to Martin and Alvar. I'll send the cassette back tomorrow. Jukka sent the sermon he preached in Borgå recently. I'd rather read the sermon than listen to the cassette.

As usual, I read Luther's sermon for today also, the 17th Sunday after Trinity. Among other thoughts, Luther used Romans 8:31, "If God is for us, who can be against us?" These words are so strong and true for me. And furthermore, "He who did not spare his own Son, but gave him up for us all—how will he not also . . . give us all things?" (Romans 8:32). Thanks be to the good Lord that we have the Word that is living and powerful.

Jukka has promised to visit me at the beginning of October. Maybe he'll be able to get to Borgå one more time before then.

We're having grand autumn weather. There's no frost yet and the trees are still green. I hope you are well and continue to be as fit as usual. I'm working with fall cleaning, and the community's cleaning crew is helping me a little.

This is a little greeting, my dear friend, "In faith, God's children are united to one."

In Jesus' name!

Ines

 Gottby ~ Monday ~ November 10
Luther's birthday

Dear Eva,

We have a new work week, and new grace that God gives us every day. They are great blessings of God as long

56

as we get out of bed every morning and begin with the forgiveness of sins each day and moment. We read in the old Catechism: "Where there is forgiveness of sins, there is life and salvation." Thank the good dear Lord in his wisdom that we are blessed children of God on account of the suffering and death of Jesus Christ, God's Son, for me, you, and the whole world. If only people would believe this and receive the gift by grace alone!

I've read in the Helsinki newspaper about the cathedral in Borgå and how learned men, pastors, and bishops argue about worldly things. Never is the Word of God mentioned. I don't know if these men are prepared to be soul caretakers for God's congregation—apparently not.

I'm sending along Jukka's cassette that I borrowed. I've listened to it many times. How rich God's Word is when a holy man of God has received grace to decipher the Word! They are men who are driven by the Holy Spirit. Now you can make a copy of the cassette and leave it for him. Even the sermons in Umeå are so good to listen to.

Jukka will tell about the church installation in Ljungby. I wonder if Seth and Birgitta traveled there?

We have been having misty and foggy weather this week. They were selling tulip bulbs for half price, so I bought a few and planted them.

I hope the pain in your shoulder is better. I'm waiting for a letter from the hospital any day now. I'll let you know the results later.

Warm greetings,

Ines

Dear Eva,

"You hem me in—behind and before; you have laid your hand upon me" (Psalm 139:5).

What grace, Eva, to be surrounded by Jesus' blessed hands every day and moment. The whole Psalm 139 has a wonderful content, rich and full of comfort for the Lord's wretched. These words are searching and life giving for all sinners in Adam's fallen family. Thanks be to the good Lord for the Word that is living and powerful!

What a festive time they had in Ljungby. The cassette recording, the song, and the music that framed Egil's sermon were good.

Yesterday, on Judgment Sunday, I heard a radio church service from Luke's congregation in Helsinki. There was an unusually good sermon by Stig Olof Fernström, who spoke about sin and grace. How seldom is the word hell used in our modern times.

Archbishop Wikström said he is leaving behind a good church in Helsinki. He is an excellent liberal in our modern time; he was satisfied with himself, but other qualities are taught about a soul caretaker by the prophet Ezekiel. The arguments going on in the cathedral in Borgå don't mention a word about sin and grace, and not one biblical passage is used in all the documents. God protect us until the end! Whether we live or die, we belong to the Lord.

Loving greetings from Ines

Dear friend Eva,

A happy new year in Jesus' name!

Thanks for the cassettes that came with the mail today. I've already listened to cassette number one, but it's difficult to understand everything. That preacher speaks so fast sometimes.

Thank you, thank you, for the telephone call just now. I took out a pen and paper to write to you. Also, thanks for the Christmas card with the friendly greetings.

"Jesus Christ is the same yesterday and today and forever." It is comforting to be able to believe this and know it is so. No matter how weak and frail we are, Jesus is the same for faithful and sinful people. The Savior Jesus was born for our sakes, and he is the Lord of heaven and earth. "Give thanks to the LORD, for he is good; his love endures forever" (Psalm 118:1).

We have so much to thank God for, especially that we are able to have our thoughts somewhat clear, and even that I can live at home as long as I have. I get a little community help two times a month. One of God's blessings is that everything is so well organized for us old folks.

Dear Eva! Whatever God has arranged or planned for us during the coming year that has just now begun, it is comforting to know that according to the words of a hymn:

> The Lord is with us, and he shall bear
> On father's arms his feeble deer.
> When earth and heaven at last shall break,
> Eternally stands our Father's word.

I thought about Pecki yesterday. It was on New Year's Day

in the evening that he moved home to the Savior. How many years ago has it been?

It is so moving to read Ola Österbacka's lectures, that I cry occasionally. May God give Ola strength to preach God's powerful works. I'll send the lectures as quickly as I can.

Loving greetings,

Ines

 Gottby ~ April 22, 1998

Dear Eva,

It's a new day, with new grace from the Lord! "The blood of Jesus Christ, God's Son, cleanses us from all sin." Thanks be to the good dear Lord who reminds us daily of this, to give us security and peace while wandering toward the goal, heaven.

Thanks for the cassette with the warm, dear greeting from old Eva in Borgå. I haven't listened to the cassette yet. Alvar speaks so quickly, as does Egil.

I thought to be out and do a little spring work. For the near future, we can expect only cold, just +3C (38F) with a thick fog. We have had a cold fog completely without the warming sun for six days. The plants outside can't sprout out of the ground and everything is held up. But the Lord gives what we need, even in regard to the material world.

The spiritual darkness, as it were, tightens even more over our country. You have surely read in the Helsinki newspaper this winter about a Finnish pastor working in Baggbole, Helsinki who has published a book in Finnish saying there is no hell. He claims that God is so good that all people go to heaven when they die, and hell exists on earth, according to him. He is able to continue with his false teaching as a youth pastor. The head cathedral says nothing, and only one official there opposed him. Many lay people have written critiques in the Helsinki paper, but no pastors. How shall this end? This is one more name to show that the Lutheran church can spread any gross false teaching at a whim.

May God preserve us in a true and living faith until the end. Maybe judgment day will come very soon. God's patience with us sinners must end. Think about the days of Lot, when Abraham prayed to God to spare the city if there were ten righteous people, but there weren't. So then came judgment, and only Lot, the righteous one, and his daughters were saved.

It was the same in Noah's time. The people lived a wild life until the flood came and washed them all away. Only Noah and those in the ark were saved.

Our days are like these times. God's Holy Word is trampled underfoot and even more delusions are spread out.

> When I in faith my Jesus see
> He becomes heartily dear to me
> Then I desire nothing more
> Than to Him be near.
> His hands and feet, his body wound
> His heart for me stands open
> There I hide both body and soul
> And feel so heartily well.

> Warm affectionate greetings,
> Ines

Dear Eva,

"The gospel is preached to the poor." Those words are from Luther's sermon today. The text is from Luke 14:16-24, Jesus' parable about a man who prepared a banquet and invited many men, but they despised the invitation and wouldn't come. So it is. The Lord Jesus invites everybody, but in our time, not many respond to Jesus' invitation. Luther says, "Christ himself is our spiritual nourishment that is put before us in the Gospel, just as he through his death completely paid for our sins and guilt and freed us from God's wrath and eternal damnation." Thank you, dear Savior! We are blessed children of God by grace, for Jesus Christ's sake.

I hope you, Eva, celebrate a happy and relaxing midsummer. We have had rain and chill here; today was only +8C (48F) with 15 mm (about ⅝ in.) of rain. There's been some warmth, but God has not yet given us a real summer's heat. Anyway, the greenery is exuberant.

I have celebrated the weekend at home, and only a few visitors who were traveling by this road came by. I thank God with all my heart that I have life so good and peaceful! Jesus' peace in the heart—who can have it better? Worries trouble me often enough, so I see for myself all the evil that we can feel as long as we are on the earth. But Jesus' victory is ours, Eva. Thanks be to the Lord!

I called Jukka before the midsummer and he plans to visit me next Sunday.

I'll write a few lines to Seth and Birgitta today.

Warm greetings,

Ines

Dear Eva,

We have a new day with new blessings from our dear Lord and Savior. Thanks for the greeting in the cassette that came yesterday. God is faithful and good! He gives us everything we need and takes care of us old folks as long as we're down here in the land of death's shadow. And then we'll have eternal life with Jesus in our heavenly home. "What eyes have not seen and what ears have not heard, that which God has prepared for us."

Thank you for your dear visit that went by far too quickly. That's a taste of what awaits us. It was fun to see each other for a little eye blink of time on earth. I received a greeting from Seth and Birgitta from Amsterdam; they were at Susanna's graduation there.

This morning we have +13C (54F). There's been sunshine and warmth for several days, a real high summer! God is still thinking of us sinners and lets the ground dry up so the late harvest can begin. Thank the good Lord!

Today I read from the letter to the Romans, the fifth chapter. What a wonderful reading, yes, all of Romans. Among other verses, here is 5:1, "Therefore, since we have been justified through faith, we have peace with God through our Lord Jesus Christ." God gives us, through his Word and Spirit, peace of heart that passes all understanding. Read this chapter, dear Eva, as a greeting from me!

Even I have been reminded how quickly this earthly life can be over. My nearest neighbor, an 81-year-old widow, lay dead in her bed one morning two weeks ago. That was a powerful reminder how life can go. The Lord alone knows each and everyone's heart.

It's been a long time now since I could get a few lines together. Everything is starting to go so slowly for me.

Loving greetings,

Ines

Epilogue

In a society where activities move so quickly and instant gratification is expected, the letters of Ines to Eva remind me that each individual can make a difference in another person's life. Both women are examples of patience in learning and practicing God's truths more deeply. Ines Lindblom and Eva Söderström, both mentally sharp but physically frail in their nineties, still encourage those around them to stay true to God's biblical teachings. Ines continues to live in the village of Gottby on Åland, an island with 26,000 people, where she stands as the lone confessional Lutheran. Eva, who began traveling to Sweden in 1978 for biblical studies in order to avoid the liberalism of the state church, thanks God for the confessional Lutheran developments in Finland. As retired pastor Jukka Söderström reports, "Mother Eva's" early work has resulted in two congregations, three pastors, one theological student, and thirty-eight members.

Karin Hokkanen
October 2002